Prayers and Meditations for Our Little Angels

**by Hafeesa Nettles
Pictures by Susan Richardson**

EWORLD INC.

**Buffalo, New York
14209
eeworldinc@yahoo.com**

Dedication

For my mother Dorrothy L. Nettles for all her support.
My sons Jalal and Tyvedokel Daaula
My sister Linda Harris and family
My sister and friend Andre Yaber
My brother and friend Alberto Cappas
My mentor and friend Alnisa Banks
My mentor and friend Leroy Baylor
My mentor and friend Mary Maybanks
My special friend, who is like a mother to me Joenetta Doggett
and lastly my editor and friend Maxwell Taylor

Prayers and Meditations for our Little Angels Text © 1996 by Hafeesa Nettles. Cover Illustration © 1996 by Chris Hall. Other Illustrations © 1996 by Susan Richardson. All rights reserved. No part of this publication may be reproduced, stored in a retrieval system or transmitted in any form by any means, electronic, mechanical, photocopying or otherwise, without first obtaining written permission from the publisher.

Library of Congress Cataloging-in-Publication Data

Nettles, Hafeesa 1954-
    Prayers and meditation for our little angels/words by Hafeesa Nettles: pictures by Susan Richardson and Chris Hall.
    p.   cm.
  Summary: Presents a collection of brief prayers, focusing on the daily concerns of young people.
    ISBN 978-1-61759-024-5
    1. Prayers-Juvenile literature.   2. Meditation-Juvenile literature.
[1. Prayer books and meditations.] I. Richardson, Susan, 1969- ill.
II. Hall, Chris, 1932- ill. III. Title.
BV265.N47   1996
242'.62-dc20   96-5895

                                                                                     CIP
                                                                                      AC

21 22 23   3 2 1
printed and bound in the United States.

EWORLD INC.

**Buffalo, New York
14209**
eeworldinc@yahoo.com

Introduction

In the south where I grew up, prayer and the acknowledgment of God's presence was taught in most households. We were taught to depend on God's Spirit that is within us

As a child, as early as age three, my parents taught me to pray. They often read me stories about God and His hosts of angels, who are always there to help us when we question anything.

My father shared with me that God is present everywhere and that he knows all things. I never understood then how this was possible, but as I grew older and actually experienced God's love and mercy, I now understand the mysteries of God's great Spirit. As I live each day I am thankful for the big blessings and the small blessings in my life.

Just as my parents shared with me the power of prayer and conversation with God, I have done the same with my two sons. I firmly believe that prayer and acknowledging God is one of life's most important foundations that parents can teach to their children...their little angels.

God is and will always be your best friend. He is always there when no one else is around. God's Spirit will allow you peace and rest when needed. God's grace will continue to awake you.daily

This book will help you to thank God for every moment of your life.

Peace and Blessings

Prayer One

*D*ear God:

At the beginning of the day when the birds begin to sing, let Your grace shower my awakening dream; and as I begin my day, stay with me from start to finish. May Your love never leave me. Thank You.

Prayer Two

Dear God:

I am told that from You all blessing flow, the blessing for my family, and for all the people that I know. Some of the blessings I see, and some I cannot see. Anyway I want to take this time to thank You for all your blessings on me.
Thank You

Prayer Three

God's Spirit who dwells in my life mystically
I come to praise Your Name, Spirit, and glory in my life
You have given to us the world, the universe.
Let my heart know Your wishes and desires for me as I live on earth
with this life You have granted me
As I seek to do Your will when my spirit meets Yours
Thank You for this present day, as You grant them one day at a time
I will trust You for my daily bread and care, through the blessing You grant me.

Forgive me for the strains I may cause to others, knowingly and unknowingly
Keep my heart clean and focus that I may stay on the straight path,
Help me to say no, to that which is not right.
Keep evil away, and my enemies abbey,
Let evil be nothing that I desire or that desires me
All power begins and ends with God
To You come all the praises and magnificence forever and always
    for only through You are all things possible.

Thank You.....Glory and Honor Always

Prayer Four
Dear God :

I understand that You have the whole world in Your hands.....
    Please, never drop me, don't let me go.
       Thank You

Prayer Five

Dear God :

Please help me to be a good child to my parents, my relatives, and my friends throughout my life, and let me grow from day to day in Your grace.
Thank You.

Prayer Six

Dear God :

Sometimes I am selfish and not satisfied with the blessings that You give me through my love ones and friends.

Although I am blessed and know that as a child I have more than many, when I ask for something and don't get it, I become testy. Help me to change, and be willing to give and not only receive. Please help me to be a person who is thankful and willing to share whatever I have.

Thank You.

Prayer Seven

Dear God:

I am young, but I can see something already that hurts me. I see homeless men, women and children. Please let the world know that we must show kindness and compassion for those who have lost their way. Lord please bless and guide the less fortunate.
Thank You.

Prayer Eight

Dear God:

Please never let me cross the thin line between love and hate. Let me only know forgiveness and love. For that is what You have always shown me.
Thank You.

Prayer Nine

Dear God:

Please help me not to form opinions against my neighbors because we may differ. You have said, "judge ye not lest you be judged".
Thank You.

Prayer Ten

Dear God:

I understand that many people have fought and died so that I may have a good education. Please guide me in my studies, and help me to understand that this is something I must do to move ahead in life. Please let me study hard because education is indeed one of Your many blessings.

Let me always remember what my ancestors, family and friends have been through just so that I might have an education.
Thank You.

Prayer Eleven

Dear God :

Pass me not, keep me by Your side. Let my heart always be humble in total submission of Your will.
Thank You.

Prayer Twelve

Dear God:

Let me be aware of all my duties from the time I rise till the end of day. Let me play when it's time to play;
Learn when its time to learn; and Love my family and friends all the time, even when I am angry.
Thank You.

Prayer Thirteen

Dear God:

Thank You for Your sunshine. It makes me very happy and is usually the sign I need to know that I am going to have a good day. Also, the sun help the flowers and the trees to grow. God, I thank You again for the sun and it's many uses. Thank You.

Prayer Fourteen

Dear God:

Thank You for the rain. I may not go out to play. But Your rain helps to wash all the dirt from the streets, and it also cleans the land. The rain also helps to grow the food that we eat. The rain gives us time to stay inside and watch television and play.
	Thank You.

Prayer Fifteen

Dear God:

Thank You for the cold weather. It may not be my favorite, but it is part of Your plan. Thank You for the warm clothes I get to wear. Thank You for the heat in my home. Thank You for all the seasons, winter, spring, summer and fall. Thank You God for creating them all. Thank You.

Prayer Sixteen

Dear God:

At times I can be very grouchy and I hurt other people's feelings. I myself don't like it when my feelings are hurt. Please help me to always be aware of what I say and do to others. And please God keep me calm even when I am not.
Thank You.

Prayer Seventeen

Dear God:

Thank You for my friends. Let us all grow in Your grace. Keep protecting us and let us always have something good to do; so that we may not become idle and get into trouble. Keep us in Your grace at all times.
        Thank You.

Prayer Eighteen
Dear God:

I am a child, but I know already what drugs and alcohol can do to families, and communities. I am asking that You somehow let the drug abusers and sellers know that this is not the right way. Let them love themselves more and seek from within a way to clean up their lives. We don't need the drugs or the alcohol. We need to have Peace and Harmony in our lives. Thank You.

Prayer Nineteen

Dear God:

You have made me different. Please don't let people be mean spirited towards me because of my color. Please make the playing field even. I believe that my mother and father have always had to work harder because of this. I feel that we are all Your children with different gifts, and talents. Don't let minds be overlooked. My ancestors have given a lot, and proven that we are a people with many abilities. And last but not least, let others be reminded that You made us all in Your Image.
Thank You.

Prayer Twenty
Dear God:

Keep my heart clean, and regenerate my spirit daily. Make me strong where I might be weak. Bless those who are sick and shut in. Let everyone know that You are the Glory, and that all things are possible with You.
Thank You.

Prayer Twenty-one
D ear God :

When I have a problem and feel that I cannot tell my mother, father, sister, brother, or friend, I know You will listen because I believe in my heart that You are always with me. Through prayer and Your guidance, I will soon share this problem with the right person.
Thank You.

Prayer Twenty-two

Dear God

Please let the only high that I receive during my life, be the high I get when I reach out to touch Your Spirit. And always guide and keep me in Your loving arms. Let Your miracles touch and deliver me, and my family, and my friends always.

Prayer Twenty-three

*D*ear God:

There are many things about today and tomorrow that I do not understand, but I know that You understand all things. You are the Creator and Knower of all. Let me understand in my heart the power of Your Spirit. When I have no answers, I know that You do. Please God, help me to follow You as a child. and as I grow older.

Prayer Twenty-four

Dear God:

Please walk with me, my family, and my friends. Protect us and guide us through every step we take. Keep all bad and evil away. Let our journey be safe whether we go far or near. Please be in our hearts always. And forever be the voice we hear.
Thank You.

Prayer Twenty-five
Dear God:

God I am tired now, my day has ended, I am going to sleep
God please watch over me and protect me
And if, You desire my soul before I wake, then I will be in Your forgiveness and Your grace.
Then I shall live with You God in Your glory and Your honor.
Thank You for loving me, my family, my friends, and the world. Thank You for being a part of my daily life. Thank You for all the blessings, the little ones and big ones, and the ones on the way. To You belong all the praise, all the honor, and all the glory. Thank You God, my prayer is done.

FINIS

I hope this book opened your eyes to the beauty of the world, and the many things you can do for yourself, your family, and the world, through prayer & belief in the Almighty GOD.

PEACE

HAFEESA NETTLES

CHILDREN'S TITLES

Fun With Series

Fun with Numbers	3.95
Fun with Letters	3,95
Fun with Colors	3.95
Fun with Shapes	3.95

Afrotots

Afrotots ABC	3.95
Afrotots 123	3.95

Other Titles

When I Look In The Mirror	6.95
When I Look In THe Mirror Coloring & Activity	2.95
Come To My Island	7.95
Prayers & Meditations for our Little Angels	8.95
Melanin & Me	6.95

Little Zeng Series

Little Zeng's ABC	4.95
Little Zeng's Ancient Egypt	2.95
Little Zeng's Hannibal	2.95
Little Zeng in Zimbabwe	2.95
Little Zeng goes to Harlem	2.95

Our Books make excellent gifts
Send for a gift Certificate and our complete catalog

EWORLD INC.
Buffalo, New York
14209
eeworldinc@yahoo.com